The Best Ever Backseat Games
Fun games to play while you are traveling

By
Michael Rist
Lene Alfa Rist

***

Copyrights © 2012
by
Michael Rist
Lene Alfa Rist

J790.1
R-15

THE BEST EVER BACKSEAT GAMES: FUN GAMES TO PLAY WHILE TRAVELING

ISBN-13: 978-1514268650
ISBN-10: 1514268655
BISAC: Family & Relationships / Activities

Authors: Michael Rist, Lene Alfa Rist
Cover Designer: Mila Perry

Danish Distribution:
Con Amore I/S
Nordre Frihavnsgade 50
2100 Copenhagen
Denmark
Phone: + 45 31 19 22 19
www.cona.dk

For information on translations or any other content related questions, please email the publisher at penhagenco@gmail.com

Fun games to play while traveling

To our families for making this book come to life. Without you this would never have been possible.

***

The best ever backseat games

Introduction

The best way to make a long trip fast and enjoyable is to keep all your friends and family entertained and laughing. But what happens when you run out of things to say or do?

You open up The Best Ever Backseat Games, the book that will make your trip unforgettable!

This book is a great way to pass time in the air, in your car or even on a train. Loaded with over one hundred games and trivia questions, this fun-packed, portable book will turn your long and exhausting trip into the best ride of your life.

The games are fun and easy to play for people of all ages. All you need is a great imagination and good sense of humor.

For a few of the games you will need a pen, a piece of paper and a few coins.

The following symbols show how many people you will need to play the games in this book.

- One or more person (no limit) ❶+

- Two people only ❷

- Two or more people (no limit) ❷+

Enjoy and have a fun time!

Table of Contents

Table of Contents

Table of Contents

Are We There Yet? ❷+

One person picks an object from a distance in the direction you are driving and says the name of the object out loud. This can be a chimney, a windmill, a road sign, or any similar object.

It is best if the object is close to the side of the road, in the direction you are driving and not too far away.

Everyone, except the driver, closes their eyes. Each person will now have to yell out "now" when they think that they have reached the agreed object. The person who is closest to the object wins.

If a person yells out "now" after you have passed the object that person is out of the game.

The person closest to the object gets one point. First person to 10 points wins the game.

Trivia: Did you know that the Hubble Space Telescope was launched into orbit by the Space Shuttle on April 24th, 1990?

Red Car – Green Car ❷+

To begin this game each person picks a color. For example, one person chooses Red and the other person selects a different color, for example, Green. (The players cannot pick the same color).

Now see if you can spot 10 cars in your respective color. You are only allowed to select cars that are driving in the opposite direction.

The first one to get to 10 cars in their respective color wins the game.

Instead of colors you can also use car brands, for example: Ford, Toyota and Audi etc.

Trivia: Did you know, according to the Guinness Book of World Records, the Toyota Corolla is the most produced car ever with over 37 million cars worldwide as of February 2011?

Let's Go Traveling ❷+

Think of a place you would like to visit. This place could be real or it could be straight from your imagination. Now use your imagination to describe what that place looks like.

Here are some suggestions to get you started:

- Is it hot or cold?
- Does it rain or is the sun always shining?
- Are there lots of buildings, mountains or trees?
- What do the people who live there look like?
- What do they do on the weekends?
- What items would you bring in your suitcase?
- How would you get there?
- How long would you like to stay?

Instead of your favorite place, you can also describe a place where you would like to send someone you don't like. Use the suggestions above to get you started.

Trivia: Did you know that there are 193 member States of the United Nations?

Counting in the Car ❶+

Find objects in the car which there are one of, two of, three of and so on. You cannot use the same object twice and you can only use items that are visible.

What is the highest number you can reach?

In the car you can find for example:

- One steering wheel
- Two front seats
- Three people
- Four doors
- Five windows
- Six speakers
- Seven knobs on the radio

Trivia: Did you know that Karl Friedrich Benz, a German engine designer and founder of the Automobile Manufacturer Mercedes-Benz, is regarded as the inventor of the first automobile powered by an internal combustion engine?

Punch Buggy ❷+

The catch in this game is to spot a Volkswagen Beetle. The person, who spots the Volkswagen Beetle, calls out; "Punch Buggy no punch backs", and hits the person closest to him on the shoulder (but not too hard).

If it was you, who called "no punch backs" no other person is not allowed to punch back.

This game can go on until you reach your destination and while you play other games.

Trivia: Did you know that the Volkswagen Beetle went into production in 1938?

Shorten the Wait Time ❶+

When you are in an airport, waiting for the bus, or waiting in line for movie tickets there are always a lot of people around you. Find a person who is not too close to you so that he or she cannot hear you.

Now make up a story about this person. See how creative you can be with your story. Below is a little inspiration for your story.

- Where does the person live?
- Sports activities?
- What is the age of the person?
- Children or grandchildren?
- Occupation?
- Best adventure?
- Crimes committed?
- Civil status?
- Hobbies?

Trivia: Did you know that the Hartsfield-Jackson International Airport in Atlanta, Georgia is the world's busiest airport?

Geography ❷+

The first person starts by picking a country which starts with the letter A, for example Argentina. The next person now has to pick a country which starts with the next letter in the alphabet, the letter B; he could for example choose, Belgium.

The next person or the first person, if you are two people playing, now has to pick a country which starts with the letter C, for example, Canada.

The person who cannot think of a country in the next order of the alphabet has lost the game.

Note: *See the reference section in the back of the book for a complete list of countries and capitals.*

Trivia: Did you know that although not a UN member state, the Vatican City is the smallest country in the world?

I Met a Man His Name Was Sam ❷+

In this game you have to make a small rhyme. The game can be played by two or more people. One person begins the rhyme by saying the first line of a rhyme that he makes up himself. He then asks any of the other players, to finish the rhyme.

The first person could for example begin the rhyme with the following line:

I met a man

The person he chooses repeats the first line and then finishes the rhyme by adding words of his own choosing that rhymes with the first line. For example:

I met a man
His name was Sam
He drank out of a bucket with both of his hands

The person, who finished the rhyme, starts a new rhyme.

Trivia*: Did you know that the earliest surviving evidence of rhyming is the Chinese Shi Jing ca. 10th century BC?*

Guess What Year ❷+

For this game you will need a handful of coins.

Put the coins close to you, but some place where you cannot see them, for example under a blanket, a pillow, or something similar.

One person places a coin in their hand and makes a fist around the coin.

Each person now takes one guess to see who can predict the year the coin was minted.

The person whose guess is closest to the year on the coin in their hand earns one point. If you guess the exact year you get double points. First person to 10 points wins the game.

Trivia: Did you know, according to the Guinness Book of World Records, the largest collection of silver coins consists of 1,600 nonduplicate coins from around the world?

The Last Tooth Pick ❷+

This little game can be played with toothpicks or any other similar objects, and is great to play if you are on an airplane or somewhere else where there is a table. To begin, place 31 toothpicks on a table.

You now take turns removing either one or two toothpicks from the table – your choice, but not more than two and at least one.

The person, who removes the last toothpick, wins the game.

If you do not have any toothpicks you can use coins or alternatively draw 31 lines on a piece of paper and then cross out the lines as you go along.

Trivia: Did you know that the oldest known archaeological fragments of the immediate precursor to modern paper date back to the 2nd century BC in China?

Ask the Professor ❷+

Start by using one of the categories below. Then agree on the number of guesses you are allowed, for example 20 guesses.

Next, choose one person to be the professor. The professor has to think of a word within the agreed category without telling anyone else the word.

Now, everyone else, who is playing, is allowed to ask the professor questions. The professor can only answer yes or no to those questions.

If no one can guess the word within the agreed number of questions the professor remains the professor and he chooses a new word.

The following are examples of categories to help you get started: Countries, Famous people, Animals, Cities, Objects in the car, Things found in a classroom etc.

Trivia: Did you know that in 2004 the movie Nutty Professor was selected for preservation in the United States National Film Registry by the Library of Congress as being culturally, historically, or aesthetically significant?

Apple Monkey Shoe ❷+

This game will test how good your memory is and is best played with three or more people. However, the game can also be played with only two people.

The first person starts by saying a word such as Apple. The next person now has to say Apple and a new word of their choosing, for example, Monkey.

The next person now has to repeat Apple and Monkey then add a new word of their choice (for example; Shoe). You continue to add a word to the list every time it is the next person's turn.

If you mess up, if you are not saying all the words in the right order or if you skip a word you are out of the game. This game can also be played in such a way that all the words have to be in a specific category such as:

- Countries, Cities, Capitals, Famous people, Boy and girl names or Animals etc.

Trivia: Did you know that apples were brought to North America by the colonists in the 17th century?

Speed Limit 100 ❷+

In this game the first person picks a number between one and ten. Then the next person adds a number between one and ten to the previous number and so on.

In this example you start with the number 7, then add a number, for example add 1, equaling 8. The next person now has to add a number to 8, for example 5. It is now the first person's turn again, and he now has to add a number to 13 and so on. The person that reaches exactly 100 wins the game.

Below is an example for the game Speed Limit 100:

Person 1	Starts with	7	Total is now	7
Person 2	Adds	1	Total is now	8
Person 1	Adds	5	Total is now	13
Person 2	Adds	9	Total is now	22
Person 1	Adds	7	Total is now	29
Person 2	Adds	8	Total is now	37
Person 1	Adds	9	Total is now	46
Person 2	Adds	3	Total is now	49
Person 1	Adds	9	Total is now	58
Person 2	Adds	8	Total is now	66
Person 1	Adds	6	Total is now	72
Person 2	Adds	6	Total is now	78
Person 1	Adds	6	Total is now	84
Person 2	Adds	3	Total is now	87
Person 1	Adds	2	Total is now	89
Person 2	Adds	2	Total is now	91
Person 1	Adds	9	Total is now	100

At the end of the game the second player adds two and gets 91. Player one can then finish the game by adding nine, thereby getting to exactly 100.

Sweet Music to My Ears ❷+

Start by humming a song. Now see if someone in the car can guess which song it is.

If nobody can guess the song you can start singing part of the song.

If nobody can guess the song after you have been both humming and singing the song you will have the option to sing another song or give your turn to the next person.

If after three turns no one can guess the song, the turn goes to the next person.

Trivia: Did you know that the television show American Idol aired on television on June 11, 2002?

What's in Your Hand? ❷+

One person starts by closing his eyes. This person is now designated the "blind person". The other person now has to put an object in the hand of the person whose eyes are closed.

The "blind person" now has to guess, keeping his eyes closed, what the object is. If he cannot guess what it is, he can then start asking yes or no questions.

He continues to ask questions until he has guessed the object.

If he cannot guess the object you start the game over with a new object.

Trivia: Did you know that Blindfold Chess is a form of chess where the two players do not see or touch the positions of the chess pieces?

Story Time ❷+

In this game you will have to make up your own story. For example: Start by telling a story about a young boy or girl who is on vacation somewhere far away. After approximately 15 seconds it is now the next person's turn to continue the story.

Keep changing the storyteller every 15 seconds or until the story comes to a natural ending.

You can also set a limit of 2 minutes to play the game.

Another way to play this game is to write down the story on a piece of paper. Each person taking turns writing one line of the story and then folding the paper, so no one knows what the other person is writing down.

You will then select a person to read the story once the page is full.

Trivia: Did you know that Hans Christian Andersen's birthday (April 2) is celebrated as International Children's Book Day?

Letter Game ❷+

This game can be played while you are sitting in the car, on an airplane, or in a restaurant, etc.

The first person has to name an object in the place you are sitting that starts with the first letter of the alphabet, e.g., the letter A.

You do not necessarily have to be able to see the object. For example, if you are driving in a car, you are allowed think of the car engine, the wheels, or the exhaust pipe and so on.

The next person now has to name an object that starts with the next letter of the alphabet, letter B, etc. You keep taking turns until someone cannot come up with a word.

You can also play this game where you are only allowed to mention things which you can see from where you are sitting.

Trivia: Did you know that the Danish alphabet is based upon the Latin alphabet and has consisted of 29 letters since 1948?

Trenton - Capital of New Jersey ❷+

This game will test how well you know the capitals of the various U.S. States.

One person is the game master. The game master can pick any state. He could for example pick New Jersey. He would then ask out loud:

What is the capital of New Jersey?

The first person who provides the correct answer gets one point. The one with the most points wins the game.

If no one can guess the capital, the game master can provide the first letter of the capital, the second letter and so on, or provide another clue of his choosing.

Note: See reference section in the back of the book for a complete list of states and capitals.

Trivia: Did you know that 70 miles of the Appalachian Trail runs through New Jersey?

Candyland ❷+

Pick a category, for example, candy. The first person now has to start by naming a piece of candy e.g. chewing gum. The next person now selects a new type of candy, for example, gummi bears.

You keep taking turns until one of the players cannot come up with another object, or one of the players say a word that has already been said.

You can also play this game using other categories such as:

- Animals
- Movies
- Vegetables
- Things in a restaurant
- Things that are red
- Things on a playground

Trivia: Did you know that cocoa originated in the Americas; however today Western Africa produces almost two-thirds of the world's cocoa?

Wordplay ❶+

For this game you will need a pen and a piece of paper. Think of a long word and write it down on a piece of paper. The word could for example be "Georgetown".

Now see how many shorter words you can make - only using letters from the chosen word. The words have to consist of at least three letters. You cannot use the letter twice in making a word, unless the letter appears twice in the original word.

From the word Georgetown you can, for example, make the following words, and many more:

- George
- Town
- Wrong
- Rent
- Tree
- Enter

It is good to set a limit for this game for example five minutes. The longer the word the longer the time limit should be.

Trivia: Did you know that the longest word in the Oxford English Dictionary is pseudopseudohypoparathyroidism and contains 30 letters?

From One to Five ❶+

This game will for sure test your math skills and is best suited for the older children. To start the game you will need a pen and a piece of paper.

Pick any number between one and one hundred, the "chosen number".

Now, use all the numbers from one to five and see if you can make them equal the chosen number. You are only allowed to use additions, subtractions, multiplications, and divisions.

For example, if the chosen number was 20 you could have the following solution:

$$3 \times 2 \times 5 - 4 - 1 = 20$$

Note: *See if you can find solutions to all the numbers from one to ten.*

Trivia: Did you know that there is no risk of lead poisoning if you stab yourself with a pencil because it contains no lead, only a mixture of clay and graphite?

From A to B ❶+

Think of different ways you can get from point A to point B. If you are traveling in a car think of ways you can get from where you live to the place you are going.

Write down how many different vehicles or other means of transportation you can think of that will take you there. Once you have written them all down you can then sort them in order from smallest to largest or in order of the fastest to the slowest.

Now share it with the rest of the people traveling with you.

Trivia: Did you know that the first man to fly solo across the Atlantic Ocean was Charles Lindbergh in 1927 and that Amelia Earhart was the first woman to fly solo across the Atlantic Ocean in 1932?

I Am Still Counting ❶+

For this game you will need a pen and a piece of paper.

There are a lot of things a person can count, when looking out the window, when they are traveling by either car, train or bus.

Each person should pick a category. The one to get to 25 items first wins the game. Below are some examples of things you can count to get you started:

- Horses
- Street signs
- Motorcycles
- Telephone boxes
- Farm houses
- Cows
- Chimneys
- Windmills

Trivia: Did you know that horses can lock the muscles in their legs so they can go to sleep standing up and not fall over?

Countries I know? ❷+

For this game you will need a pen and a piece of paper.

The object of this game is for each person to write down as many countries as possible on a piece of paper.

The person with the most countries wins the game. Before you start this game you and your partner should agree on how much time you have, to write down all the countries, for example; two minutes.

This game can also be played with other categories such as:

- Rivers
- Cities
- Capitals
- Cars
- Animals
- Movies

Note: See the reference section in the back of the book for a complete list of countries and capitals.

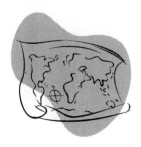

Trivia: *Did you know that the river Nile is the longest river in the world?*

Famous People ❷+

The first person starts by saying the first and last name of a famous person, for example, Michael Jackson.

The next person now has to say the name of a famous person whose first name starts with the first letter in Michael Jackson's <u>last</u> name.

In this example the first letter in Michael Jackson's last name is the letter J. The next person could then think of James Bond. It is now the first persons or the next persons turn, if played by more than two people, to name a famous person whose first name starts with the letter B, for example, Betsy Ross.

If the famous person's first and last name starts with the same letter the direction reverses. Note, this is only relevant if the game is played by more than two people.

The "famous person" has to be known by at least one other person playing the game. If that is not the case the person will need to explain what this person has done to be famous.

Trivia: Did you know that Betsy Ross is widely credited with making the first American flag?

I Know More Than You ❷+

For this game you will need a pen and a piece of paper.

Pick a letter in the alphabet for example, the letter E. You now have two minutes to see who can list the most famous people whose name starts with the letter E.

The one who writes down the most people wins the game. If the first and last name starts with the same letter you get double points.

You can also select other categories instead of famous people such as:

- Boy and girl names
- Animals
- Movies
- Vegetables
- Things in a restaurant
- Things that are red
- Things on a playground

Trivia: Did you know that the last name "Smith" is one of the most common surnames in the United States?

I Am Just The Opposite ❷+

In this game one person will have to name the opposite of the word the other person is saying. You are only allowed to name a word where you can name the opposite word yourself.

See how many different things you can come up with.

Here are some examples to get you started:

- Light / Dark
- In / Out
- Cold / Warm
- Black / White
- Sun / Moon
- Summer / Winter

Trivia: *Did you know that Yang is the white side with the black dot, and Yin is the black side with the white dot?*

Funny Face ❶+

For this game you will need a pen and a piece of paper.

Draw three lines on a piece of paper or draw a letter in the alphabet, for example, the letter A.

Now ask the other person to draw a face incorporating the three lines you started out with, or the letter you drew on the paper earlier. You can make up lots of very funny faces.

You can also select animals that you have to draw instead of faces, however, this is much more difficult.

Trivia: Did you know that the NATO Phonetic Alphabet is the most widely used spelling alphabet?

Fun games to play while traveling

Turn Up The Volume ❷+

Play some music on the radio, CD player or iPod etc., for a couple of seconds and then turn down the volume.

Now see who can guess which song it is that is playing.

You will have to guess it before the song is over. If no one can guess the song you can turn up the volume a little longer so that they can hear more of the song.

If no one can guess the song you skip to the next one.

Trivia: Did you know that the first iPod was released in 2001?

Sing a song for me ❷+

In this game the first person starts by singing the first five words of a song. The next person now has to sing the following five words.

To make the game easier you can choose to have the next person only say the next word in the song.

The best way to play this game is to use songs that most players know. In order to play this game the person choosing the song has to know the words the other person has to sing.

Trivia: Did you know that Bob Dylan's song Desolation Row, written in 1965, is 11:21 minutes long?

Fun games to play while traveling

If I Were President ❷+

This game is fun to play with the younger children.

If you were the King or the President of a country what three things would you change and why?

This can be the start of a really good discussion.

Take turns once the first person is done.

Trivia: Did you know that Woodrow Wilson was President of Princeton University and also President of the United States?

Cities and States ❷+

The first person starts by naming a city, for example, Princeton.

The next person now has to name a city that starts with the last letter of the city the first person named. Since the letter N is the last letter in Princeton. He could, for example, say New York.

It is now the first persons turn again and he has to name a city that starts with the letter K and so on. You can also play this game with categories such as:

- Capitals
- Boy and girl names
- Things in a restaurant
- Things that are red
- Things on a playground

Trivia: Did you know that the Statue of Liberty was a gift to the United States from the people of France?

Car Roulette ❷+

This game can only be played when you are traveling by car. You will need a piece of chalk or some tape to play this game.

Take a piece of chalk and write your initials on one of the car tires. If you do not have chalk, then take a piece of tape, write your initials on it, and tape it onto one of the tires.

Now make a mark with either chalk or tape above the tire (on the body of the car). Next time you stop to get gas or food see whose initials are closest to the mark.

The person closest to the mark wins the game.

If you do not want to mark the car you can determine the winner by the one whose initials are closest to the ground.

Trivia: Did you know that the wheel in French/European roulette has 37 colored and numbered pockets, whereas there are 38 colored and numbered pockets on the American roulette wheel?

Hold Your Breath ❶+

In this game you will test how long you can hold your breath.

You can play this game with more people and compete on who can hold their breath the longest.

This game can be played anywhere, but is most fun when played in the water.

Trivia: Did you know, according to the Guinness Book of World Records, that the longest time someone held their breath underwater was 20 minutes and 21 seconds?

Make Me Laugh ❷

This game is best played by only two people. Sit down across from each other. Now take turns trying to make the other person laugh without using any words and without touching the other person.

You have two minutes to make the other person laugh. If you do not succeed it is now the other persons turn to try to make you laugh.

Trivia: Did you know that the study of humor and laughter, and its psychological and physiological effects on the human body, is called gelotology?

I Spy ❷+

This is a great game to play while you are traveling in a car especially, if you are in a city with lots of things to look at. However, you need to make sure that you can continue to see the object as long as you play the game.

The first person starts by saying, for example, "I spy with my little eye a blue elephant". The other players now have to find the blue elephant which in this example could be on an advertisement poster.

Once one of the other players has found the object, it is now his turn to spy something.

Do not make the object too difficult to find. Finding the object easily and taking turns going back and forth makes a fun game.

Trivia: Did you know that the International Spy Museum is located in Washington, D.C.?

Guess What Animal ❷+

In this game the first person thinks of an animal and tells the rest of the players the first letter of the animal. The other players now take turns guessing what animal it is by asking only yes or no questions.

The only questions you are <u>not</u> allowed to ask, is if the next letter is the letter a, b, c and so on.

Once one of the other players has guessed the animal they have won the game. The winner of the game chooses the next animal. If no one can guess the animal he can give out the next letter. He should continue to give out letters until someone has guessed the animal.

Here are some questions to ask to get you started:

- Does it have four legs
- Is it bigger than my hand
- Does it live in the water
- Does it live in Africa
- Is it brown

Trivia: Did you know that the blue whale is believed to be the largest mammal ever to have lived?

Alternative Energy ❷+

Pick an object, such as a paper cup, a coaster, a napkin, a straw or any other object that you have with in your reach. Now come up with alternative use for this object e.g., the paper cup. Only your imagination limits you in this game.

You can play this game by taking turns or you can write the alternatives down on a piece of paper to see who can come up with the most alternatives.

Once you run out of ideas pick another object. This game is also fun to play when you are in a restaurant waiting for the food.

Below are some examples of what a paper cup can be used for.

- Plant holder
- Pencil holder
- Party hat
- Small drum if turned upside down

Trivia: Did you know that the world's largest "paper" cup is made of concrete, and is about 68.1 feet tall, and located in Riverside, California?

What Has Changed ❷+

Sit or stand across from the other person. One person has to close his eyes. While that person's eyes are closed, the other person has to change something visible on themselves, for example removing his glasses.

The first person now has to open his eyes. Within one minute he now has to guess what the other person has changed. Here are some examples to get you started:

- Remove glasses
- Put your watch on the other hand
- Remove jewelry

If you are two or more people playing the game, then have the third person make the change on the other person.

Trivia: Did you know that in the movie "American Graffiti" the license plate on Richard Dreyfuss car is changed every time it is shown?

Klunse ❷+

This game is played with coins or any other small objects that you can conceal in your hand. It's pretty simple, each player has to use three coins each.

Let us assume that this game is played by two people, however, there is no limit to the number of people who can play the game. Each person takes three coins (or three other small objects) in their hand and places both hands behind their back.

With both hands behind their backs, under the table, or somewhere not visible to the other players, each person takes either zero, one, two or three coins and places them in the right hand (the playing hand). When everyone is ready to play they place the playing hand in front of them. The hand needs to be closed so the other people cannot see how many coins you have selected, if any. The left hand stays behind the back.

The object of the game is to guess the combined number of coins in all the playing hands. You have one turn each and you cannot say the same number. If no one guesses the right number you start over again. If one of the players guesses the right number, he removes one of his coin, so that he only has two coins left to play with and so on. The first person to get rid of all three of their coins wins the game. You take turns going first after each round.

Trivia: Did you know that there is 293 ways to make change for a dollar?

Say Something ❷+

Before you start the trip each person traveling writes a word or a sentence down on a piece of paper. Without showing it to anyone else put the paper in the glove compartment or somewhere else where nobody can see it.

The purpose of this game is to get one of the other passengers to say the word you wrote down out loud, while incorporating it into a normal conversation and before you get to your destination.

Once you get to your destination, everyone tries to see if they can guess the word that was written on the paper and the word they were supposed to say.

If there are more than three people traveling you can also exchange the word that someone else wrote down, this will make it a lot funnier and a lot more difficult.

Trivia: Did you know that no word in the English language rhymes with month, orange, silver or purple?

Honk Your Horn ❷+

This game can be played when you are driving in a car and have stopped at a red light. Each player guesses how long it will take for the car behind you to honk his horn if you do not immediately start driving when the light turns green.

Be careful here and do not hold up the traffic too long.

Trivia: Did you know that Cape Horn is the southernmost point of the continent of South America and is named (indirectly) after the Dutch town of Hoorn?

Picture Game ❶+

For this game you will need a pen, a piece of paper as well as a magazine or newspaper.

Take a page out of the magazine or newspaper, preferably a page with a lot of pictures or a lot of details.

Now look at the page for 15 seconds and then turn the page with the back side facing up.

Take a separate piece of paper and write down all the things you remember from the page. The person who has the most things written down wins the game.

To make the game easier or more difficult you can increase or decrease the time allowed to look at the page.

Alternatively, using only one page by all players, you take turns naming something on the page, if you guess incorrectly you are out of the game.

Trivia: Did you know that Time Magazine's "Man" of the Year in 1982 was the Personal Computer?

Prices On The Menu ❷+

This game is fun to play when you are in a restaurant. Before you get the menu (or with only one person looking at the menu) guess what items are the most and least expensive.

You can also play this game by guessing the price of your favorite menu food or favorite drink. The person closest to the real price wins the game.

You can also try to guess what the total amount of the dinner is going to be while you are waiting for the bill. The one furthest from the total, picks up the tab.

Trivia: Did you know that the first American restaurant to use printed menus was Delmonico's Steak House in New York City in 1837?

Coin Toss ❷+

This game can be played when you are in a restaurant waiting for your food, or somewhere else where there is a table.

Each person takes a coin and places it on the table. Put the coin so that a little piece of the coin is over the edge of the table.

Now tapping the coin once with only your finger nail, see who can get the coin closest to the other end of the table.

The one closest to the edge wins the game. If your coin falls off the table you have lost the game. If your coin is over the edge, but still on the table you get two points.

First one to five points wins the game. If you have a lot of time to spare you play to ten.

Trivia: Did you know that a dime has 118 ridges around the edge?

Guess Who I Am ❷+

The first person has to think of a famous person without telling anyone who it is.

He now has to start sharing information about this person, while the other people try to guess who it is.

The first person could for example think of Santa Claus. He could then slowly give out one clue at a time revealing the following information:

- I am a man
- I have a big belly
- I have a beard
- I like to make people happy
- I like animals
- I like Christmas a lot

Trivia: Did you know that in some European countries children receive their presents on St. Nicholas' Day, either the 6th or 19th of December?

Another Meaning ❷+

For this game you will need an old book or some printed pieces of paper.

Before you start your journey take out a couple of pages of an old book you do not care to keep anymore. Alternatively you can also print out a couple of pages from the internet before you start your trip, or use the pages in this book.

Now everyone, who is not driving, circles words on their own page. Once everyone has finished circling words, read each circled word in the order it was circled to create a whole new sentence.

You can make up some really funny sentences or stories.

Trivia: Did you know that the Bible is the most sold book worldwide?

Ghost ❷+

In this game the first person starts by thinking of a word. He should not share this word with any of the other players. He now has to say the first letter of the word out loud. For example, if the first person choses the word Banana, then the first letter would be the letter B (which is now locked in).

The next person now has to think of his own word that starts with the letter B, which could be Book. He now has to say the first and second letter "BO" of his word out loud. It is now the first person's turn or the next person's if played by more than two people. The first word does not matter anymore. He now needs to think of a word that starts with BO (the locked in letters). The word that he thinks of could be Bold.

He now has to say "BOL" out loud. The next person now has to think of a word that starts with BOL (the locked in letters). If he cannot think of any word that starts with BOL he can pretend to have a word and say a random letter, but if he gets caught he loses the game.

If he does not believe that there is a word that starts with BOL he calls out the person that said the letters and asks him to say his word. If he was not making up something and is actually saying a real word such as BOLD he wins the game – if not he caught and loses the game.

If any of the players say out loud a real word consisting of four or more letters that player has lost the game.

Trivia: Did you know that the movie Ghostbusters was the highest-grossing comedy of all time, until the release of the movie Home Alone?

The Price Is Right ❷+

This game is best played with three or more people.

One person picks something on the menu and the other person has to guess the price of that item. The one closest to the price wins the game and it is now his turn to pick a new item.

If only played by two people, the person who picks something from the menu gives three suggestions as to the price of the item. The other player now has to guess which one of the three suggestions is the right one.

This game can also be played with picking three items on the menu and then having everyone else guess the order of the three items from the cheapest to the most expensive, or the reverse.

Trivia: Did you know that the current version of the television program "The Price is Right" premiered on 4 September 1972 on CBS?

Draw Your Hands ❶+

For this game you will need a pen and a piece of paper.

Trace your hand on a piece of paper. Now see how many different faces or people you can create by drawing eyes, nose, and ears etc., on each of the fingers.

Trivia: *Did you know that the human hand has 27 bones?*

Fun games to play while traveling

Come to China ❷+

In this game the first person thinks of a rule without telling anyone else what the rule is. He then applies this rule when he says "You can come to China if you bring?"

For example, he could make the following rule: All things have to be red. He will then start the game by saying "You can come to China if you bring strawberries". The other people playing the game have to figure out the rule by asking the following question "Can I come to China if I bring?"

The next person will then say "Can I come to China if I bring a dog" The first person will then say "No" because a dog is not red. The first person will then give out the next clue by saying "You can come to China if you bring an apple?"

The second person now might think that the rule may be fruit and he asks; "Can I come to China if I bring a banana?" The first person will then say "No", because a banana is typically not red.

The first person will give the next clue by saying "You can come to China if you bring a fire truck?" The next person might now know that the rule has to do with something red and he asks "Can I come to China if I bring a red hat?" and the first person says "Yes". The first person to guess the rule wins the game.

Trivia: Did you know that China's population is more than 1.355 billion, the largest of any country in the world?

The Bus Stop ❶+

This game can be played be one or more people.

If you are traveling by bus try and guess how many people get on the bus next time you stop.

If there are several stops before you get to your destination you can play several rounds.

You can also guess how many people get off the bus. However, this is a little more difficult to count as there are often a lot of people rushing to get off the bus.

You can also play this game on the train.

Trivia: Did you know, according to the Guinness Book of World records, that the most people crammed on an unmodified bus is 229 and was achieved by the Faculty of Mechanical Engineering of the Krakow University of Technology in Krakow, Poland, on 1 June 2011?

Survival Game ❷+

It is always hard to figure out what to bring with you when you are traveling. Most often you bring a lot of stuff you never need such as, too many shirts, too many books etc.

However, the fewer items you are allowed to bring the more difficult it is. If you were only allowed to bring five items with you, what five items would you bring if you were going to?

- Africa
- A deserted island
- The North Pole
- Running out of a burning house
- Away to boarding school

Trivia: Did you know that the Swiss Army knife was first produced in 1891?

Spelling Game ❷+

This game can be played by two or more people.

Start by spelling a word one letter at the time. Now see who can guess the word the fastest. You will have to spell out the word slowly and pick age appropriate words.

First person to ten right guesses wins the game, if played be two or more people.

Trivia: Did you know that the first National Spelling Bee Competition was held in Washington, D.C. in 1925?

Design Your House ❷+

Some people like to change around their rooms, make changes to their house, basement and so on.

If you were to design your own house what would it look like? Here is a little inspiration for your new house.

- Locations
- Rooms
- Garden
- Swimming pool
- Neighbors
- Horses
- Secret rooms

Trivia: Did you know that Burj Khalifa also known as Burj Dubai, in Dubai, United Arab Emirates is the tallest artificial structure in the world, standing at 829.8 meter?

I'm a Millionaire ❷+

Only a few people are so lucky to win the lottery. However, if you won a Million dollars what would you spend it on? Below are some questions to get you started with the game?

- What you would buy?
- To whom would you give money?
- Who would you buy presents for?
- How much would you put in the bank?
- Where would you hide your money?

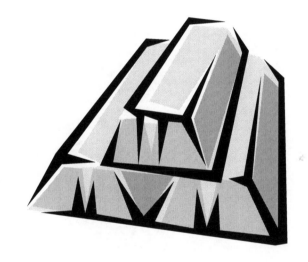

Trivia: Did you know that the largest U.S. Lottery Jackpot was $640 million, won on 30 March 2012?

The Movie Director ❷+

If you were the director of a new movie, what movie would you make?

- What would the movie be about?
- Who would be in the movie?
- Where would it take place?
- Would it be an action, comedy or drama?

Tell your story with as many details as possible. Try to incorporate the other people traveling with you, your destination, and your hometown and so on.

Trivia: Did you know, according to the Guinness Book of World Records, that the most films seen in one year is 1,132 and was achieved by Maggie Correa-Avilés in San Juan, Puerto Rico, from 1 January 2010 to 31 December 2010?

The Spelling EEB ❷+

Spell a word backwards one letter at the time and see who can guess what word it is. The first one to guess the word wins the game.

Start with easy words and progress slowly to more difficult words.

Listed below are a few fun words that will help you get started.

These words all have a different meaning when spelled backwards. These types of words are called palindromes and were coined by Martin Gardner.

- Stressed
- Stop
- Snap
- Evil
- Star
- Diaper

Trivia: Did you know that the word "Stewardesses" is the longest word that is typed with using only the left hand on a standard keyboard?

Abbreviations Anyone? ❷+

Every day we are surrounded by more and more abbreviations from the government, the news and from the use of smart phones. In this game you take turns saying out loud an abbreviation for something that you use in your everyday life. Now see if the other person can guess what it is.

You can say it has to be in a specific category such as school related, business related, something you write in a text message, etc.

Here are a few abbreviations just to get you started.

- BFF (Best Friends Forever)
- CIA (Central Intelligence Agency)
- FBI (Federal Bureau of Investigation)
- UN (United Nations)
- ROFL (Rolling on Floor Laughing)

Trivia: Did you know that Martin Cooper made the world's first handheld cellular phone call in public on April 3, 1973, when he called Joel S. Engel at the New York Hilton with a two-pound Motorola DynaTAC phone?

What Came First ❷+

Here is a fun game to play with the younger children. Ask them what came first?

- The automobile or the horse?
- The chicken or the egg?
- The CD player or the VCR?
- The cow or the milk?
- Adam or Eve

Now have the person explain why he thought that the chosen items came first.

Trivia: Did you know that a chicken egg takes 21 days to hatch?

Yellow ❷+

For this game, everyone in the car agrees on a color, in this example the color agreed on is the color "yellow".

From now on, whenever a yellow car is seen, someone shouts - Yellow! Whoever shouts out "Yellow!" first, gets a point.

You can count your "points" or you can just play and estimate who has the most "points" at the end of the trip.

You can continue this game until you reach your destination and while you are playing other games.

Trivia: Did you know that white is the most popular color for new cars, according to the 2012 DuPont Automotive Color Popularity Report?

Christmas Trees ❶+

When you are out driving in December, there are always a lot of Christmas trees around.

See how many Christmas trees with lights on you can find. Every time you spot a Christmas tree you get one point. The one with the most points wins the game.

You can also play against each other, with one person counting all the Christmas trees on the left side and the other person counting all the Christmas trees on the right side. One point for each tree, the one with the most points wins the game.

Trivia: Did you know that the Christmas tree traditionally was decorated with edibles such as apples, nuts, or other food items?

One Little Lie ❷+

This game is fun to play when you are driving with people who do not know each other very well. The first person starts by telling three stories about himself. Two of the stories have to be true and one of the stories has to be a lie.

The object of the game is now for the other players to guess which story is a lie.

Note, it is most fun if all the stories are somewhat similar, either all very believable or all unbelievable. However, don't make you lie too obvious.

Trivia: Did you know that the polygraph was invented in 1921 by John Augustus Larson, a medical student at the University of California at Berkeley and a police officer of the Berkeley Police Department in Berkeley, California?

Billboards ❶+

When you are traveling on the highway there are always a lot of billboards around.

In this game you will have to find separate billboards with words containing the letter A, B, C and so on, in the order of the alphabet.

See if you can get through the whole alphabet before you get to your destination.

Trivia: Did you know that there are more than 500,000 billboards on U.S. highways?

License Plates ❶+

In this game you will have to find license plates from different U.S. States on cars traveling in the opposite direction of where you are going.

See if you can find a license plate from each of the 50 U.S. States.

If more than one person is playing this game you can write them down and see who can find the most different license plates in 10 minutes.

Note: See the reference section in the back of the book for a complete list of the 50 U.S. States and State Capitals.

Trivia: Did you know that there are more than 250 million passenger cars in the United States according to a recent survey by the Department of Transportation?

Rocks Paper Scissors ❷

This is the classic game of Rock Paper Scissors and can be played by two people only. The game is often used as a method similar to coin flipping.

The players count aloud "Rock, Paper, Scissors, Go". On "Go" the players show their hand with one of three gestures and extend it towards their opponent. The gestures are:

- Rock (represented by a closed fist)
- Paper (represented by an open hand)
- Scissors (represented by two fingers extended)

The objective is to select a gesture which defeats the other player. Gestures are resolved as follows:

- Rock crush (defeats) scissors
- Scissors cut (defeats) paper
- Paper covers (defeats) rock

If both players choose the same gesture, the game is tied and the players go again. Best out of three wins the game.

Trivia: *Did you know that Pumice is a volcanic rock and the only rock that can float in water?*

Fast Food Anyone? ❶+

There are over 160,000 fast-food restaurants in America. Can you think of one that starts with the letter A, B, C and so on?

Take turns naming a fast-food restaurant. If the game is played by two or more people. First person not being able to name a fast-food restaurant, repeating one or simply naming a restaurant that is clearly is not a fast-food place, is out of the game.

Now see if you can get through the entire alphabet before you reach your destination.

Trivia: *Did you know that fast food restaurants serve more than 50 million Americans daily?*

The Muppet Show ❷+

One person in the car names a character from a famous television show or movie, for example "Kermit", from the Muppet Show.

He says out loud "In what television show or movie can you find Kermit".

Now the other people in the car have to guess the name of the television show or the movie in which Kermit is a character.

If the other person cannot easily guess the television show or movie, the person who has named the character can start giving out clues. The clues can be in form of the first letter, the second letter and so on. Other clues can also be given out one at the time; for example, the shows contain a very angry pig, a Swedish cook and so on.

Trivia: Did you know that Kermit the Frog was first introduced in 1955 by Jim Henson?

Cows and Horses ❷+

This game can be played with two or more people.

When driving in the country side one person pick horses and the other person pick cows.

Now see who can find the most horses or cows, first person to 25 wins the game. If you do not get to 25 within five minutes, then the person who has spotted the most wins the game.

Trivia: Did you know that there are about 920 different breeds of cows in the world?

What Did You Say? ❷+

Most license plates have a combination of numbers and letters. By only using the letters, see if you can come up with a sentence that match the letters on the license plate.

For example, if the license plate on the car in front of you is:

<u>WAM</u> 25 <u>H</u>

You can for example come up with the following sentence:

<u>W</u>ho <u>A</u>te <u>M</u>y <u>H</u>otdog?

You can play this game with cars that are passing you or cars that you are passing.

Trivia: Did you know that in Hawaii, the license plates have a unique letter designation based on the island counties that residents purchased or registered the vehicles from?

Scavenger Hunt ❶+

Write down on a piece of paper 20 different objects before you start your road trip. The objects should be things that can somewhat easily be spotted on your road trip.

During the road trip each person now has to find the listed objects. The one with the most objects spotted wins the game.

Note: See the reference section in the back of the book for a detailed list of scavenger hunt examples.

Trivia: Did you know that the movie "Pirates of the Caribbean" had its first release on the big screen in 2003?

Guess That Movie ❷+

In this game the first person says a line or quote from a famous movie, television show or commercial out loud.

It could be "May the Force be with you".

The other people in the car now have to guess what famous movie, television show, or commercial the line is from.

In this example the line "May the Force be with you", is from the movie Star Wars.

Note: See the reference section in the back of the book a detailed list of famous Movie Quotes.

.

Trivia: Did you know that Clint Eastwood is a certified pilot?

Fizz Buzz ❷+

Fizz Buzz is best played with more than three people but can also be played with two people. This game will for sure test your skills about division.

Players take turns to count incrementally, replacing any number divisible by seven with the word "Fizz", and any number containing the number seven with the word "Buzz". If the number is both divisible by seven and contains the number seven, the player will say "Fizz Buzz" and the order changes directions.

For example 1, 2, 3, 4, 5, 6, "Fizz Buzz" 8, 9, 10, 11, 12, 13 "Fizz", 15 16 "Buzz", 18, 19, 20, "Fizz", etc.

There are many variations of this game. You can substitute seven with any other number or you can change "Fizz" or "Buzz" with any other word.

Trivia: Did you know that seven has the highest probability of occurring as an addition when rolling a pair of dice?

You Said What? ❷+

In this game you have to come up with words that that are spelled the same, but have different meanings. For example, the word bat has more than one meaning. It means a wooden bat you hit a baseball with, and it can also mean an animal that flies around at night.

The first person thinks of a word that is spelled the same, but has a different meaning. He then says it out loud. The first person who can come up with the other meaning of the word wins the round and it is now his turn to come up with a new word that meets the above definition.

Trivia: Did you know that a Homonym is a word that sounds alike but has a different meaning? Homophones are a type of homonym that also sound alike and have different meanings, but different spellings. Homographs are words that are spelled the same but have different meanings.

Car Manual Quiz ❷+

The Car Manual Quiz is a chance to finally learn what is in the owner's manual of your car. Everyone can take turns being the quiz master.

The quiz master flips through the car manual and finds something interesting that he can turn into a true or false question. For example: True or False: The hand break needs to be engaged when you are changing a flat tire?

The quiz master selects a person to answer the question. The player answers true or false and the quiz master tells them if they are right or wrong.

Each right question is worth one point. First one to ten points wins the game.

Trivia: Did you know that Matchbox cars was introduced by Lesney Products in 1953? The company is now owned by Mattel, Inc.

Word Play ❷+

This game will for sure test your creativity.

In this game each player writes down ten words on a piece of paper. Each player then exchanges paper with someone else so that no one ends up with their own paper.

Now everyone has five minutes to come up with a story using all ten words. Once the time is up each person takes turn reading their story.

Trivia: Did you know that there's an Ernest Hemingway lookalike society that holds yearly contests?

The Glass Is Half Empty ❷+

In this game you have to change a negative statement to something positive. As a wise man once said you can always find something positive in everything and everyone.

The quiz master starts by making a statement such as: Unfortunately, we just had a flat tire and everyone now needs to get out of the car.

The quiz master selects the person who has to make this statement into something positive.

The person could for example say: "That is great, then we get to stretch our legs for a little bit".

After his statement has been made, he is now the quiz master and it is now his turn to come up with a new statement starting with; "unfortunately".

Trivia: Did you know that the Pacific Ocean, at 165.25 million square kilometers, is the largest of the Earth's oceanic divisions?

Mix and Match ❷

In this game you mix and match two categories. Each player picks a category. First player could for example pick countries as a category and the second player could for example pick girls names.

To play the game, the first player names a country, for example, Argentina. The next person now has to name something from his own category that starts with the last letter of the word the first person named.

Using the last letter in Argentina, he could say for example; "Anne". It is now the first persons turn. Using the last letter in Anne, he could for example say England.

You can mix and match any two categories. The following are a few examples to get you started: Food and boy names, Countries and things in the car, Girl names and famous people, U.S. States and famous athletes, Cities and television shows etc.

Trivia: Did you know, according to the Guinness Book of World Records, the jigsaw puzzle with the most pieces consisted of 551,232 pieces and was completed by 1,600 students of the University of Economics of Ho Chi Minh City in Vietnam, on 24 September 2011?

The Human Skeleton ❷+

Did you know that there are 206 bones in the human skeleton?

Take turns naming a bone in the human skeleton. The first one to get stuck loses the game.

This game is much more difficult than you think. Can you name more than three, five or ten?

Trivia: Did you know that the animal with the strongest bones in the entire world is the blue whale?

U.S. State Capitals ❷+

This game will test your knowledge of U.S. State Capitals.

Take turns naming a U.S. State Capital. First one to get stuck, repeating a capital or naming an incorrect capital, is out of the game. Last man standing wins the game.

Note: *See the reference section in the back of the book for a complete list of count U.S. State Capitals.*

Trivia: Did you know that in 1959 Alaska and Hawaii became the last two states to join the USA? They are also the only ones not connected to the other 48 states.

Landmarks ❷+

The Landmark game is fun to play and will test everyone's knowledge about geography.

One person is the game master. The game master starts by picking a landmark, for example, Stonehenge. He then asks the other players the following question:

Where is Stonehenge located or in what country do you find the landmark Stonehenge?

First person to guess the right answer, gets one point. First person to ten points wins the game.

Trivia: Did you know that there were two types of stones used at Stonehenge? The larger sarsens, and the smaller bluestone.

Waiting for the Train ❷+

This game is fun to play if you are stuck on the road waiting for the train to finish crossing the road you are traveling on.

It is best played if you are at the crossing before the train starts arriving.

While the cross bars are going down each person in the car yells out the total number of cars including the locomotive there are on the train.

Person to get closest to the exact number of cars wins the game.

Trivia: Did you know that there is over 209,308 railroad crossings is the U.S. as of July 2014 and that railroad crossings exist in all 49 continental U.S. States, with the leading five states being Texas, Illinois, California, Kansas and Ohio?

Three of a Kind ❷

Starting with the letter A, each person tries to be the first to spot and name three items beginning with the letter A. This could for example be:

- Apple tree
- Audi station wagon
- Automatic seat warmer

The first person to spot and say out loud three items, wins the game and is rewarded the opportunity to pick the next letter.

Trivia: Did you know that a Royal Flush is the best possible hand in standard five-card Poker?

Driving in Reverse ❷

This game is best played with two people only.

First player say a list of five random words. The other person now has to repeat these five words in reverse order.

For example; the first player could say:

- Apple, Window, Tree, Street, Mailbox

The second player now has to say:

- Mailbox, Street, Tree, Window, Apple

If the opponent succeeds he wins the game and it is now his turn to come up with five new words.

Trivia: Did you know that the automatic transmission was introduced back in 1939?

Tic Tac Toe ❷

This game is a popular paper-and-pencil game for two players.

First draw a grid as shown on the picture.

First player places an X on the grid. Second player plots an O.

Players continue to take turns until one player has three across. First player to have three across in any direction wins the game.

Trivia: Did you know that an early variant of Tic-Tac-Toe, called Terni Lapilli, was played in the Roman Empire, around the first century BC?

Connect the Dots ❷+

Connect the Dots is a pencil and paper game for two players. The game works best when each player uses a different colored pencil or pen, for example, red and blue or two other contrasting colors.

First draw a grid, made of dots, as shown on the picture below.

Starting with an empty grid of dots, players take turns, adding a single horizontal or vertical line between two unconnected adjacent dots.

A player who completes the fourth side of the box earns one point and takes another turn. (The points are typically recorded by placing, in the box, an identifying mark of the player, such as an initial). The game ends when no more lines can be placed.

The winner of the game is the player with the most points.

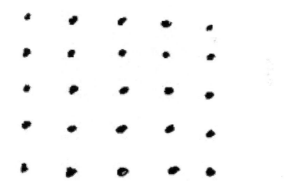

Trivia: Did you know that there are 1,048,576 pixels in a Megapixel, calculated as 2 to the power of 20?

Telephone ❷+

This game is best played with as many people as possible but no less than two people.

First person whispers a story to someone else in the car. That person whispers the same story as close to a word for word recount as possible, to a third person, and so on.

The last person to hear the story repeats it out loud so everyone can hear.

Invariably, some of the story will have been lost in the translation, and the resulting garbled message usually inspires a good laugh.

Trivia: Did you know that "lost in translation" is the title of a movie, released September 12, 2003 about a lonely, aging movie star named Bob Harris (Bill Murray) and a conflicted newlywed, Charlotte (Scarlett Johansson)?

Tongue Twister ❷+

Here are a couple of tongue twisters that should be a challenge for most people.

Try saying really fast any of the following:

- One smart fellow he felt smart, two smart fellows they felt smart, three smart fellows they all felt smart

- Quick kiss, quicker kiss

- Red leather, yellow leather

- Clean clams crammed in clean cans

Trivia: Did you know that the tongue is often referred to as the strongest muscle in the human body? The tongue is actually comprised of eight different muscles that provides it with a wide range of movement. The tongue is also the only muscle that is connected at only one end?

Traffic Light ❷+

When you are stopped at a red light take turns guessing how many seconds it will take before it turns green.

Trivia: *Did you know that on December 9th, 1868 the first non-electric gas lit traffic lights were installed outside the British Houses of Parliament in London?*

References

List of items for scavenger hunt

Airplane

Airport sign

Ambulance

Barn

Bicycle on the back of an RV

Billboard

Bird

Black car

Blue car

BMW

Bridge

Broken tail light

Burger King

Camping ground

Car stop on the side of the road

Cat

Cell phone tower

Christmas tree

Church

Cows

Dog

Electric fence

Exit sign

Farm house

Fire truck

Gas station

Goat

Greyhound bus

Horse

Horse trailer

Kids in the back seat

Lake

Limousine

Mail truck

McDonalds

Motorcycle

Pedestrian walk

Person running

Police car

Power lines

Purple car

Red car

Rest area

River

Roof rack

Sign with speed limit 35

Snowman

Stop sign

Supermarket

Tandem bicycle

Taxi

Tent

Tow truck

Toyota Corolla

Tractor

Traffic light

Trail

Trees

Truck

Water tower

Waterfall

White car

Windmill

Wooden fence

Yellow school bus

Yield sign

List of countries and capitals

Abkhazia	Sukhumi
Afghanistan	Kabul
Akrotiri and Dhekelia	Episkopi Cantonment
Albania	Tirana
Algeria	Algiers
American Samoa	Pago Pago
Andorra	Andorra la Vella
Angola	Luanda
Anguilla	The Valley
Antigua and Barbuda	St. John's
Argentina	Buenos Aires
Armenia	Yerevan
Aruba	Oranjestad
Ascension Island	Georgetown
Australia	Canberra
Austria	Vienna
Azerbaijan	Baku
Bahamas	Nassau
Bahrain	Manama
Bangladesh	Dhaka
Barbados	Bridgetown
Belarus	Minsk
Belgium	Brussels
Belize	Belmopan
Benin	Porto-Novo
Bermuda	Hamilton
Bhutan	Thimphu
Bolivia	Sucre
Bosnia and Herzegovina	Sarajevo
Botswana	Gaborone
Brazil	Brasília
British Virgin Islands	Road Town

List of countries and capitals

Brunei	Bandar Seri Begawan
Bulgaria	Sofia
Burkina Faso	Ouagadougou
Burma	Naypyidaw
Burundi	Bujumbura
Cambodia	Phnom Penh
Cameroon	Yaoundé
Canada	Ottawa
Cape Verde	Praia
Cayman Islands	George Town
Central African Republic	Bangui
Chad	N'Djamena
Chile	Santiago
China	Beijing
Christmas Island	Flying Fish Cove
Cocos (Keeling) Islands	West Island
Colombia	Bogotá
Comoros	Moroni
Cook Islands	Avarua
Costa Rica	San José
Croatia	Zagreb
Cuba	Havana
Curaçao	Willemstad
Cyprus	Nicosia
Czech Republic	Prague
Democratic Republic of the Congo	Kinshasa
Denmark	Copenhagen
Djibouti	Djibouti
Dominica	Roseau
Dominican Republic	Santo Domingo
East Timor (Timor-Leste)	Dili
Easter Island	Hanga Roa

List of countries and capitals

Ecuador	Quito
Egypt	Cairo
El Salvador	San Salvador
Equatorial Guinea	Malabo
Eritrea	Asmara
Estonia	Tallinn
Ethiopia	Addis Ababa
Falkland Islands	Stanley
Faroe Islands	Tórshavn
Federated States of Micronesia	Palikir
Fiji	Suva
Finland	Helsinki
France	Paris
French Guiana	Cayenne
French Polynesia	Papeete
Gabon	Libreville
Gambia	Banjul
Georgia	Tbilisi
Germany	Berlin
Ghana	Accra
Gibraltar	Gibraltar
Greece	Athens
Greenland	Nuuk
Grenada	St. George's
Guam	Hagåtña
Guatemala	Guatemala City
Guernsey	St. Peter Port
Guinea	Conakry
Guinea-Bissau	Bissau
Guyana	Georgetown
Haiti	Port-au-Prince
Honduras	Tegucigalpa

List of countries and capitals

Hong Kong	Victoria City
Hungary	Budapest
Iceland	Reykjavík
India	New Delhi
Indonesia	Jakarta
Iran	Tehran
Iraq	Baghdad
Ireland	Dublin
Isle of Man	Douglas
Israel	Jerusalem
Italy	Rome
Ivory Coast	Yamoussoukro
Jamaica	Kingston
Japan	Tokyo
Jersey	St. Helier
Jordan	Amman
Kazakhstan	Astana
Kenya	Nairobi
Kiribati	Tarawa Atoll
Kosovo[g]	Pristina
Kuwait	Kuwait City
Kyrgyzstan	Bishkek
Laos	Vientiane
Latvia	Riga
Lebanon	Beirut
Lesotho	Maseru
Liberia	Monrovia
Libya	Tripoli
Liechtenstein	Vaduz
Lithuania	Vilnius
Luxembourg	Luxembourg
Macedonia	Skopje

List of countries and capitals

Madagascar	Antananarivo
Malawi	Lilongwe
Malaysia	Kuala Lumpur
Maldives	Malé
Mali	Bamako
Malta	Valletta
Marshall Islands	Majuro
Mauritania	Nouakchott
Mauritius	Port Louis
Mexico	Mexico City
Moldova	Chisinau
Monaco	Monaco
Mongolia	Ulaanbaatar
Montenegro	Podgorica
Montserrat	Plymouth
Morocco	Rabat
Mozambique	Maputo
Nagorno-Karabakh Republic	Stepanakert
Namibia	Windhoek
Nauru	Yaren
Nepal	Kathmandu
Netherlands	Amsterdam
New Caledonia	Nouméa
New Zealand	Wellington
Nicaragua	Managua
Niger	Niamey
Nigeria	Abuja
Niue	Alofi
Norfolk Island	Kingston
North Korea	Pyongyang
Northern Cyprus	Nicosia
Northern Mariana Islands	Saipan

List of countries and capitals

Norway	Oslo
Oman	Muscat
Pakistan	Islamabad
Palau	Ngerulmud
Panama	Panama City
Papua New Guinea	Port Moresby
Paraguay	Asunción
Peru	Lima
Philippines	Manila
Pitcairn Islands	Adamstown
Poland	Warsaw
Portugal	Lisbon
Puerto Rico	San Juan
Qatar	Doha
Republic of the Congo	Brazzaville
Romania	Bucharest
Russia	Moscow
Rwanda	Kigali
Sahrawi Arab Democratic Republic	El Aaiún
Saint Barthélemy	Gustavia
Saint Helena	Jamestown
Saint Kitts and Nevis	Basseterre
Saint Lucia	Castries
Saint Martin	Marigot
Saint Pierre and Miquelon	St. Pierre
Saint Vincent and the Grenadines	Kingstown
Samoa	Apia
San Marino	San Marino
Saudi Arabia	Riyadh
Senegal	Dakar
Serbia	Belgrade
Seychelles	Victoria

List of countries and capitals

Sierra Leone	Freetown
Singapore	Singapore
Sint Maarten	Philipsburg
Slovakia	Bratislava
Slovenia	Ljubljana
Solomon Islands	Honiara
Somalia	Mogadishu
Somaliland	Hargeisa
South Africa	Pretoria
S. Georgia & the S. Sandwich Islands	King Edward Point
South Korea	Seoul
South Ossetia	Tskhinvali
South Sudan	Juba
Spain	Madrid
Sri Lanka	Sri Jayawardenepura Kotte
State of Palestine	East Jerusalem
Sudan	Khartoum
Suriname	Paramaribo
Swaziland	Mbabane
Sweden	Stockholm
Switzerland	Bern
Syria	Damascus
São Tomé and Príncipe	São Tomé
Taiwan	Taipei
Tajikistan	Dushanbe
Tanzania	Dodoma
Thailand	Bangkok
Togo	Lomé
Tonga	Nuku'alofa
Transnistria	Tiraspol
Trinidad and Tobago	Port of Spain
Tristan da Cunha	Edinburgh of the Seven Seas

List of countries and capitals

Tunisia	Tunis
Turkey	Ankara
Turkmenistan	Ashgabat
Turks and Caicos Islands	Cockburn Town
Tuvalu	Funafuti
Uganda	Kampala
Ukraine	Kiev
United Arab Emirates	Abu Dhabi
United Kingdom	London
United States	Washington
United States Virgin Islands	Charlotte Amalie
Uruguay	Montevideo
Uzbekistan	Tashkent
Vanuatu	Port Vila
Vatican City	Vatican City
Venezuela	Caracas
Vietnam	Hanoi
Wallis and Futuna	Mata-Utu
Yemen	Sana'a
Zambia	Lusaka
Zimbabwe	Harare

List of best picture Oscar winners

2013	12 Years a Slave
2012	Argo
2011	The Artist
2010	The King's Speech
2009	The Hurt Locker
2008	Slumdog Millionaire
2007	No Country for Old Men
2006	The Departed
2005	Crash
2004	Million Dollar Baby
2003	The Lord of the Rings: The Return of the King
2002	Chicago
2001	A Beautiful Mind
2000	Gladiator
1999	American Beauty
1998	Shakespeare in Love
1997	Titanic
1996	The English Patient
1995	Braveheart
1994	Forrest Gump
1993	Schindler's List
1992	Unforgiven
1991	The Silence of the Lambs
1990	Dances With Wolves
1989	Driving Miss Daisy
1988	Rain Man
1987	The Last Emperor
1986	Platoon
1985	Out of Africa
1984	Amadeus
1983	Terms of Endearment
1982	Gandhi
1981	Chariots of Fire
1980	Ordinary People

List of best picture Oscar winners

1979	Kramer vs. Kramer
1978	The Deer Hunter
1977	Annie Hall
1976	Rocky
1975	One Flew over the Cuckoo's Nest
1974	The Godfather Part II
1973	The Sting
1972	The Godfather
1971	The French Connection
1970	Patton
1969	Midnight Cowboy
1968	Oliver!
1967	In the Heat of the Night
1966	A Man for All Seasons
1965	The Sound of Music
1964	My Fair Lady
1963	Tom Jones
1962	Lawrence of Arabia
1961	West Side Story
1960	The Apartment
1959	Ben Hur
1958	Gigi
1957	The Bridge on the River Kwai
1956	Around the World in 80 Days
1955	Marty
1954	On the Waterfront
1953	From Here to Eternity
1952	The Greatest Show on Earth
1951	An American in Paris
1950	All About Eve
1949	All the Kings Men
1948	Hamlet
1947	Gentleman's Agreement
1946	The Best Years of Our Lives

List of best picture Oscar winners

1945	The Lost Weekend
1944	Going My Way
1943	Casablanca
1942	Mrs. Miniver
1941	How Green Was My Valley
1940	Rebecca
1939	Gone with the Wind
1938	You Can't Take It with You
1937	The Life of Emile Zola
1936	The Great Ziegfeld
1935	Mutiny on the Bounty
1934	It Happened One Night
1933	Cavalcade
1932	Grand Hotel
1931	Cimarron
1930	All Quiet on the Western Front
1929	The Broadway Melody
1928	Wings

List of Roman Numerals

I	1	XXXIV	34
II	2	XXXV	35
III	3	XXXVI	36
IV	4	XXXVII	37
V	5	XXXVIII	38
VI	6	XXXIX	39
VII	7	XL	40
VIII	8	XLI	41
IX	9	XLII	42
X	10	XLIII	43
XI	11	XLIV	44
XII	12	XLV	45
XIII	13	XLVI	46
XIV	14	XLVII	47
XV	15	XLVIII	48
XVI	16	XLIX	49
XVII	17	L	50
XVIII	18	LI	51
XIX	19	LII	52
XX	20	LIII	53
XXI	21	LIV	54
XXII	22	LV	55
XXIII	23	LVI	56
XXIV	24	LVII	57
XXV	25	LVIII	58
XXVI	26	LIX	59
XXVII	27	LX	60
XXVIII	28	LXI	61
XXIX	29	LXII	62
XXX	30	LXIII	63
XXXI	31	LXIV	64
XXXII	32	LXV	65
XXXIII	33	LXVI	66

List of Roman Numerals

LXVII	67	C	100
LXVIII	68	M	500
LXIX	69	D	1000
LXX	70		
LXXI	71		
LXXII	72		
LXXIII	73		
LXXIV	74		
LXXV	75		
LXXVI	76		
LXXVII	77		
LXXVIII	78		
LXXIX	79		
LXXX	80		
LXXXI	81		
LXXXII	82		
LXXXIII	83		
LXXXIV	84		
LXXXV	85		
LXXXVI	86		
LXXXVII	87		
LXXXVIII	88		
LXXXIX	89		
XC	90		
XCI	91		
XCII	92		
XCIII	93		
XCIV	94		
XCV	95		
XCVI	96		
XCVII	97		
XCVIII	98		
XCIX	99		

List of U.S. Presidents

1. George Washington (1789-1797)
2. John Adams (1797-1801)
3. Thomas Jefferson (1801-1809)
4. James Madison (1809-1817)
5. James Monroe (1817-1825)
6. John Quincy Adams (1825-1829)
7. Andrew Jackson (1829-1837)
8. Martin Van Buren (1837-1841)
9. William Henry Harrison (1841)
10. John Tyler (1841-1845)
11. James K. Polk (1845-1849)
12. Zachary Taylor (1849-1850)
13. Millard Fillmore (1850-1853)
14. Franklin Pierce (1853-1857)
15. James Buchanan (1857-1861)
16. Abraham Lincoln (1861-1865)
17. Andrew Johnson (1865-1869)
18. Ulysses S. Grant (1869-1877)
19. Rutherford B. Hayes (1877-1881)
20. James A. Garfield (1881)
21. Chester Arthur (1881-1885)
22. Grover Cleveland (1885-1889)
23. Benjamin Harrison (1889-1893)
24. Grover Cleveland (1893-1897)
25. William McKinley (1897-1901)
26. Theodore Roosevelt (1901-1909)
27. William Howard Taft (1909-1913)
28. Woodrow Wilson (1913-1921)
29. Warren G. Harding (1921-1923)
30. Calvin Coolidge (1923-1929)
31. Herbert Hoover (1929-1933)
32. Franklin D. Roosevelt (1933-1945)
33. Harry S Truman (1945-1953)

List of U.S. Presidents

34. Dwight D. Eisenhower (1953-1961)
35. John F. Kennedy (1961-1963)
36. Lyndon B. Johnson (1963-1969)
37. Richard Nixon (1969-1974)
38. Gerald Ford (1974-1977)
39. Jimmy Carter (1977-1981)
40. Ronald Reagan (1981-1989)
41. George Bush (1989-1993)
42. Bill Clinton (1993-2001)
43. George W. Bush (2001-2009)
44. Barack Obama (2009-present)

List of U.S. States and Capitals

Alabama	Montgomery
Alaska	Juneau
Arizona	Phoenix
Arkansas	Little Rock
California	Sacramento
Colorado	Denver
Connecticut	Hartford
Delaware	Dover
Florida	Tallahassee
Georgia	Atlanta
Hawaii	Honolulu
Idaho	Boise
Illinois	Springfield
Indiana	Indianapolis
Iowa	Des Moines
Kansas	Topeka
Kentucky	Frankfort
Louisiana	Baton Rouge
Maine	Augusta
Maryland	Annapolis
Massachusetts	Boston
Michigan	Lansing
Minnesota	St. Paul
Mississippi	Jackson
Missouri	Jefferson City
Montana	Helena
Nebraska	Lincoln
Nevada	Carson City
New Hampshire	Concord
New Jersey	Trenton
New Mexico	Santa Fe
New York	Albany

List of U.S. States and Capitals

North Carolina	Raleigh
North Dakota	Bismarck
Ohio	Columbus
Oklahoma	Oklahoma City
Oregon	Salem
Pennsylvania	Harrisburg
Rhode Island	Providence
South Carolina	Columbia
South Dakota	Pierre
Tennessee	Nashville
Texas	Austin
Utah	Salt Lake City
Vermont	Montpelier
Virginia	Richmond
Washington	Olympia
West Virginia	Charleston
Wisconsin	Madison
Wyoming	Cheyenne

List of Movie Quotes

I'm king of the world!
Titanic
You had me at "hello."
Jerry Maguire
You can't handle the truth!
A Few Good Men
Hasta la vista, baby.
Terminator 2: Judgment Day
If you build it, he will come.
Field of Dreams
Snap out of it!
Moonstruck
I feel the need - the need for speed!
Top Gun
Go ahead, make my day.
Sudden Impact
E.T. phone home.
E.T. The Extra-Terrestrial
Here's Johnny!
The Shining
Toga! Toga!
National Lampoon's Animal House
You talking to me?
Taxi Driver
Is it safe?
Marathon Man
You're gonna need a bigger boat.
Jaws
Keep your friends close, but your enemies closer.
The Godfather II
Soylent Green is people!
Soylent Green

List of Movie Quotes

You've got to ask yourself one question: 'Do I feel lucky?
Dirty Harry

I'm walking here! I'm walking here!
Midnight Cowboy

Open the pod bay doors, HAL.
2001: A Space Odyssey

What we've got here is failure to communicate.
Cool Hand Luke

Mrs. Robinson, you're trying to seduce me. Aren't you?
The Graduate

A martini. Shaken, not stirred.
Goldfinger

A boy's best friend is his mother.
Psycho

I have always depended on the kindness of strangers.
A Streetcar Named Desire

Made it, Ma! Top of the world!
White Heat

Who's on first.
The Naughty Nineties

Play it, Sam. Play 'As Time Goes By.'
Casablanca

Oh, Jerry, don't let's ask for the moon. We have the stars.
Now, Voyager

Frankly, my dear, I don't give a damn.
Gone With the Wind

After all, tomorrow is another day!
Gone With the Wind

Oh, no, it wasn't the airplanes. It was Beauty killed the Beast.
King Kong

Listen to them. Children of the night. What music they make.
Dracula

List of Movie Quotes

Elementary, my dear Watson.
The Adventures of Sherlock Holmes
Show me the money!
Jerry Maguire
Houston, we have a problem.
Apollo 13
There's no crying in baseball!
A League of Their Own
I'll have what she's having.
When Harry Met Sally
Greed, for lack of a better word, is good.
Wall Street
Nobody puts Baby in a corner.
Dirty Dancing
I'll be back.
The Terminator
Say "hello" to my little friend!
Scarface
They're here!
Poltergeist
I love the smell of napalm in the morning.
Apocalypse Now
May the Force be with you.
Star Wars
I'm as mad as hell, and I'm not going to take this anymore!
Network
Yo, Adrian!
Rocky
Attica! Attica!
Dog Day Afternoon
Forget it, Jake, it's Chinatown.
Chinatown

List of Movie Quotes

I'm going to make him an offer he can't refuse.
The Godfather

Love means never having to say you're sorry.
Love Story

Get your stinking paws off me, you damned dirty ape.
Planet of the Apes

Hello, gorgeous.
Funny Girl

We rob banks.
Bonnie and Clyde

Gentlemen, you can't fight in here! This is the War Room!
Dr. Strangelove

Bond. James Bond.
Dr. No

Well, nobody's perfect.
Some Like It Hot

Fasten your seatbelts. It's going to be a bumpy night.
All About Eve

What a dump.
Beyond the Forest

Louis, I think this is the beginning of a beautiful friendship.
Casablanca

Round up the usual suspects.
Casablanca

The stuff that dreams are made of.
The Maltese Falcon

There's no place like home.
The Wizard of Oz

As God is my witness, I'll never be hungry again.
Gone With the Wind

It's alive! It's alive!
Frankenstein

List of Movie Quotes

Mother of mercy, is this the end of Rico?
Little Caesar
Wait a minute, wait a minute. You ain't heard nothin' yet!
The Jazz Singer
Mama always said life was like a box of chocolates. You never know what you're gonna get.
Forrest Gump

The best ever backseat games

***

Index

Index

F

G

H

I

Index

Index

S

T

U

Index

W

Y

The best ever backseat games

PENHAGENCO LLC

***

Page | 129

Made in the USA
San Bernardino, CA
29 October 2016